Reaching Peckham

a story in 40 poems

Hylda Sims

Hearing Eye

Published by Hearing Eye 2009

Hearing Eye
Box 1, 99 Torriano Avenue
London NW5 2RX, UK
email: books@hearingeye.org
www.hearingeye.org

All trade orders to: Central Books, 99 Wallis Road, London E9 5LN

Poems © Hylda Sims, 2009   www.hylda.co.uk
ISBN: 978-1-905082-45-2

Four of the poems in *Reaching Peckham* appeared in *Sayling the Babel*
(Hearing Eye, 2006)

I would like to thank Susan Johns, John Rety and Martin Parker for their
help in making this book possible, and Sharon Morris for the drawings used
on the title and final pages. I would also like to thank the readers, musicians
and recording engineers (referred to in detail in CD notes) who did much of
the work on the CD of *Reaching Peckham* which is available with this book
and from www.hylda.co.uk – Hylda Sims

Printed and bound by Imprintdigital.net
Designed by Martin Parker at www.silbercow.co.uk
Cover artwork by Martin Parker
Drawings by Sharon Morris

For Viv, Rom, Lily, Wilfe, Rufus & Remus

&

In memory of Southwark Individual Tuition Centre at Meeting House Lane, Peckham

It is said that, after sacking Roman London, Queen Boudicca and her warriors lost their last battle on Peckham Rye where Boudicca killed herself.

It is said that William Blake, as a child, saw a tree of angels on Peckham Rye.

In the Domesday book, Peckham is known as Pecheham. Perhaps Meg Peach's ancestors lived there.

Reaching Peckham is a set of poems which together make a story. Its characters range from reclusive poet Oliver to illiterate teenager and leader of the Angels gang, Mehmet. Their linked stories are told through the eyes of a third character – Oliver's friend, Mehmet's teacher – Lorna.

The story is distilled from a novel of mine, *Divs and Poets*, and is also about the process of writing fiction.

Reaching Peckham concerns the life and landscape of a maligned inner-London suburb in the mid-1990s.

It was set to music, recorded and performed at the Dulwich Festival and on the London Fringe in 1996 by

the Boudicca Band:
>Dave Arthur, Sarah Barton, Serge Gorlin, Susumu Ishida, Warabe Tatekoji and Guy Whitby

with readers
>Tony Butten, Michael Hallam, Bron Jones, Simon Ings and Liz Simcock

it was produced and directed by
>Lucien Crofts and Hylda Sims

recording was by
>Gary J Brady of Escapade Recording Studio, Greenwich

A CD of this original recording, re-mastered by Andrew Thompson of Sound Performance, Greenwich, is available with (or without) this book.

Hylda Sims

Contents

Reaching Peckham

INTRO

I'm coasting into Peckham
lowlights reflecting
on my graphite wings

at the hospital
ambulances flashing
a bleeping on the wind,

above the Sally Army building
obelisks prod me
towards heaven

I bank over the station,
tiny drinkers by the Phoenix
toy trains rattling

follow the railway down
sketch in the nick, the pickle factory
(a whiff of onion)

Rye Lane is a red necklace
of buses, pavements beaded
with bargain shoppers

stalls down Choumert Road send up
a flare of foreign fruits,
turbulence of Reggae rocks me

Concrete dominoes stack
little terraces fold away
behind me

The Rye, a grassy tablecloth,
sets out its vegan banquet
warm air holds me, I glide

a flock of geese
a crimson kite
join me in the sky

BLURB

'A virgin poet's hard to find... she pushed him down
silently removed his new clean clothes
slowly raised her arms
her bead top floated down
landed with a shucking sound
slowly she bent down
removed her stout black boots
removed her matt black tights
she had nothing more to lose'

> Meet gorgeous goth Yula, who
> with her bewitching kiss, transforms
> Oliver – (solitary, overweight
> he dare not think of girls, for him
> eating is like aspirin) to Oscar:
> that name fell round him like a well-cut suit
> declared him poet laureate of Peckham

'William Blake woz 'ere, here on the Rye
he saw a tree of angels, he had visions
long gone now, but Mehmet's heard of him
the school was on a local history project
before he got excluded, yeah, kicked out, for punching
Mr Gabriel, codenamed Muscles'

> Meet Mehmet's Angels: tiefers, motor nickers
> neighbour hasslers, blammers, jungle blasters
> hanging round the Burlington Estate
> where Oliver sits, puzzling out pentameters
> blockaded in his top floor council flat
> on the walkway...confetti of lottery tickets
> spaghetti of graffiti...in the streets...
> tin banks of knackered cars...

MEET THE AUTHOR

Lorna
guitar toting
hash smoking
acid dropping
nineties dropout
runs the Drop-in Centre
down in Peckham
might drop everything
for a nice new man
watches
listens
from her semi
on the rim
Mehmet's teacher
friend of Oliver
first person
unwrapping them...

a landscape...

story...

ONE

...characters

Oliver

They come in different transports
Olly on his pre-cred trainers, drifting
through a swirl of rainbow leaves
humping those bags of his, heavy
with unsung verse and Kwik Save bargains
giant cola, jumbo packs of chips

Trips into Lorna's armchair, spills the milk,
slops his mug of lapsang, deftness stranded
on the inside, his outside barges on
without its engine, foots warily through tunnels
of other people's domesticity

See him now, blinking at the crossroads
where Rye Lane's cut price pavements bustle by
the ancient common land
farthingales of willow shade the Lido
old man's beard wraps round the rails
six seasons' leaves are rotting
in the deep end, spiked they say with bones
of Boudicca, her rebel hordes
a scent of peat and battle filters through the fence
once Blake sat dreaming here, a host of light
glancing through a skirt of pale green leaves

Mehmet

     crashes in by car
another Angel riding shot
parks the motor

somewhere round the back
one more Angel watches out for bill
Mem ain't taking

any chances; drops in round
the Centre for a while
He don't read much

shies off books as others
back away from bombs or
growling dogs, grumbles

This is boring Miss,
let's cook, play pool
this lesson's rubbish

Angels Triolet

The Angels loiter by the Butcher's Arms
(they're underage, but... well)
in triolet they clock the bagman
while loitering by the Butcher's Arms.
He's by the Jade Star Chinese, at the bus stop...
That geezer, what's he wearing!

The Angels laugh and fall about
still loitering by the Butcher's Arms
underage, but what the hell

Carpentry   Lorna

and me here
not sure
       how rain came on, what dampened
grumbled in unclear skies, worried the days
then sudden and cold, hammered the town,
       about my lost lover, his sour, stubborn chatter
then laughter rinsing down, bleaching his words
I liked his workman's hands turning the lathe

not sure
       how love came on, what quickened,
his blunt fingers flowing on my skin
while he flattened my house with lumpen blows,
       about hate, the sullen streaming of it
hate's from the heart, love's closer to the bone

I'm not sure
       how he cramped and turned my feet
or how I chiselled free, alone, in the rain

The Others...

Yula hovers over Peckham
invisible to Olly
polishing her spell
of sharp white teeth
and purple fingernails
teasing out her wands
of raven hair

* * *

Landed from the moon
heavenly music beaming in his ears
tendons winged, body smooth'd in Lycra
on silver spokes, in mask and shining helmet
leaving the Crystal Palace on the skyline
a meter reader cycles down through Forest Hill

* * *

Muscles ticked them off with a sharp red mark
in those corporal days
first lesson, shirt off, turned his back
arms up, for inspection
Muscles' back had muscles
most pupils understood the implications
he'd spin and catch some bother smirking at the back
one lunge, two earlobes, *Got it?*
Muscles wasn't nasty, just knew how it had to be
for him, for them

Muscles has kept up to date, he has the jargon:
this term's report –
Mehmet's reading is sub-phonic, but he calculates...
with digital support ...
Muscles is an educated man
respects the laws of gravity
knows that being down is heavy
shoot up high enough you'll float
Muscles is no masochist, he's hard
calculates his scale points in his head

* * *

Meg Peach ain't too old to down a stout
in the Wishing Well. Let her start:
There used to be a blacksmith's down Rye Lane
where that Bigger Burger Bar now stands
I was in service, big place over Nunhead
course, them days that was open land

all them rooms and beds, and 'Morning Marm'
for bed and board and three and six a week
Sundays after church, I'd meet my Tom
up One Tree Hill, that's how I fell with Albert
just before the war, no one could tell
all them years, you can't believe it can you

Good boy Albert, brings me of a Friday
going on for eighty, never wed
war baby, him, his dad got left in Mons
full of mustard, steel bolt in his head
The regulars nod, 'Come on Mum it's time',
Bert tucks her rug in, wheels his ma back home

TWO

Olly's Verses

neither seen nor heard
longing to sing out, neglected
lark about his skimpy place all day
Olly earns their keep as best he can
working as a packer down at Argos

returning via Iceland
up the walkways, past
Peckham Angels chanting
Mister ain't you married?
What are you – some poofter?
Past the smoked-up chipboard
of the flat next door

He hardly gets inside
before they nag at him, his own
creep out of dirty washing in the doorways
droop across the bathroom floor
fall off his unmade bed
spin him round like spiders

immaculate conceptions in shoeboxes
scribbling on the kitchen walls
ballades on the backs of bills
clerihews on old newspaper
villanelles on bean tin wrappers
a word-infested wasteland
in Peckham's upper air

Someone's at the door, blond ponytail
(social worker, canvasser?)
 flashes his ID with picture, surveys the kitchen
toast-shards crunching underfoot
assassinates a cockroach...
I've come to read the meter

and invite you to the club
Peckham Poets, at the Butcher's Arms
on Mondays – why not take them out
poor things, banged up here indoors
prisoners of consciousness
self-consciousness...
I write myself a bit, I know what's good ...

Mehmet at the Centre   Cooking with Lorna

Eggs on target, spludge! Causing a flourstorm.
Sugar hails down, pounds, sweet shrapnel
saturation milk bombing, splunge! Dropscones

      Sideways large at thirteen, Mehmet
      tee by Disney, knuckle rings, his feet
      go East West – Mecca, McDonald's

      His dad, crazy for sea, for Famagusta palms
      shouts *You're a fool Mehmet, how is this?*
      Your father's a wise man and wallops him

Splutch! In the big cast iron skillet
lava islands of lumpen batter spread
blue smoke rises *Turn down the gas, Mem*

he turns the scones, squodge! Flup!
they shoot out legs, running, charred on top
Mehmet lands two, stuffs one in his mouth

Look out, they're hot! Don't matter,
he crams the other. Splotch! More mixture seethes
Mehmet! (he's dripped across the cooker)

Yesterday, computers: mousing the screen with
fabulous fonts, he copies fifty times
(*Stop, stop Mehmet!*) KEEP YOUR KITChEN CLEAN, writ Gothic

I'd tacked up this advice, while he played pool
The white escaped at once into a pocket, reds
dived overboard, obscenities fizzed out:

'Your mum's, up your mum's
up your fucking mum's'... *Mehmet!*
'...vagina... it's a word, innit?'

Mehmet off the Burlington, down Peckham,
wears granny's *nuska* on his full pink breast
she has no charms to ward off God, his dad

He grabs the bowl, tips it all, splurch... ch... ch!
The scorching skillet bubbles to the rim
Mem, be careful! smoke obscures the Gothic

lava belches, heaves, resists cremation
spatulas flail, we heft it, spitting, dripping,
spladge! You have half, goes Mehmet, kind

Home time, budge. He wants to stay
smacking pool balls down, battering the black moon
great sweet scones feeding his famished heart

Oliver Goes Out   (unusual for him)

Olly edged between the pleat-and-button
simulated leather seats (all ripped)
with caution, Angels thronged the poolroom
he did his best to tiptoe up the stairs

people chatting in a semi-circle
smell of stale hops stored in beige wallpaper
on it stills of Millwall players, signed.
Are you a reader? His tacky notebook quivered
What's your name?   *Good one for a poet!*

'Oscar Peckham' – the name fell round him, fitted
covered his awkwardness, his Oxfam bags;
it wasn't till he stood to read, faced them
that he saw her, with her pint jar, at the back:

      Ears, nose, arms, fingers
      all of them were ringed with silver
      butterflies rested on her shoulder
      her hair was wild and black, opaquely thick
      some strands were overlaid in purple braids
      which hung about her head like floating fronds
      of petal cloth, fringed her smooth
      white-painted cheeks, themselves a canvas
      for her big brown almond-sat-in eyes
      which matched her umber love-boat mouth –
      it tipped and smiled, Oscar's only wish
      to drown between her gleaming coral teeth

There was a hollow silence in the room
an anti-wind
had sucked out all the sound
siphoned it outside
tap tap of someone's stick along Rye Lane
bus doors whooshing closed
laughter by the Jade Star Takeaway
banter from the bar
bubbling up the stairs
bursting by the door

a hollow silence in the room
everyone waited
to hear the space injected
with Olly's high-pitched nasal stammer
he blinked *Don't blink*
groaned Oscar prodding in the backbone
Go!

A deep, compelling voice he didn't know
rang out – the rest he can't remember...
the air repopulating, shouts of
Oscar – More! More!
He thought they were applauding
a striker from the pictures on the wall
and then, her sepia print upon his cheek
We love you Oscar, you're our poet
...coffee...next week... at the squat...?

Gypsy, Queen   Lorna remembers

Traveller, trader, singer, signer
count the plumstones on my plate
golden-band-men, one-night-stand-men
breathing sighs and pulling strokes

preacher, teacher, social worker
count the words like falling stones
put-things-right-men, talk-all-night-men
making rules for other folks

banker, broker, wheeler-dealer
count the gemstones in their ties
mobile-phone-men, can't-get-home-men
keeping wives in Sevenoaks

brickie, chippie, handyperson
count the grindstones in the shed
up-at-dawn-men, mow-the-lawn-men
raising beans and artichokes

actor, author, TV talker
count the signs in Waterstones
make-a-name-men, come-to-fame-men
striking poses, telling jokes

drummer, strummer, penny-whistler
count the time like rolling stones
R & B men, fast and free men
splicing spliffs and taking tokes

Lady, baby, gypsy, queen
count the milestones down the lane
not one plum left on the platter
what became of all those blokes ?

Mehmet and the Angels

What shall we do today
break in and drive away
Underneath the forward wheels we cut out the alarm
tap in with a T-hammer it don't do too much harm
a little bit of know-how and we're flying like a bomb
What shall we do today
take it and drive away!

THREE

What does one wear for coffee at a squat? – Olly turns to
Lorna for guidance

Getting Kitted

He got the money as I told him to, five hundred
Fixed his pocket with two safety pins, slid
the fifties in. We met at two, in Covent Garden
Can you imagine what a mess he looked, those trainers!
Generations had inhabited his suit –
who wears suits? We went straight to Marks and Spencer

(first things first) eight pairs of jockey shorts (one spare)
and sixteen pairs of socks, he changed his underwear
in Covent Garden toilets, most convenient (can't
imagine where he put the old stuff) then
to Boots for nail file, comb and condoms, fragrances
then round the men's boutiques, 'John', 'Jools', and 'Jim'

I made him buy a dark green shirt with just a hint
of check, he said it needed ironing (get him!)
navy cotton chinos, best not to match too much
What a change, can you imagine! He fumbled out
two hundred quid; I made him pose and turn and strut
look in the mirror (I do believe he's getting thinner)

Worst things last: the trainers - a really sweet assistant
rather camp, binned them obligingly, straight-faced
brought back a pair of absolutely stunning plimmers
plain black, only fifty notes, can you imagine
what Olly said! *Oh Lorna – just like school, from Woolworths*
I'm glad we're only friends – what would you do with him?

Yula knows what to do with him, and how, and where...

At the Squat

On the hills
below the Crystal Palace
the decorous follies
of Victorians
calling out for servants

      to feather brush
      their egg and arrow cornices
      scrub the flowering tiles
      below rich marble mantels
      polish up with leather
      shining ruby panes
      of panelled doors, leading
      past anaglypta dados
      massage lovingly
      the handsome newel post
      run a duster round
      a hundred curling spindles
      and shake the beds
      in every draughty
      heavy-curtained room;
      who drudge and dream, while
      Marm takes tea
      and sometimes laudanum
      where gillieflower and hollyhock
      medlar, persimmon and pear
      stretch on the wall –

have now turned into squats:

ethereal scarves
        of candle smoke
        jasmine oil and joss
        diffuse and float
        by plaster fruit and flowers
        long composted under
        layers of gloss
        the fireback
        is fleecy soot;
        upstairs
        Crapper's pale blue porcelain roses
        in a crazed bowl
        are mulched and watered
        frequently
        behind a door
        without a handle;
        people settle
        onto floorboards, mention
        marij, thin cheroots
        home grown
        where thistles bloom
        in gardened mattresses –

the houses stand   watch...

A Virgin Poet's Hard to Find

Olly felt at home
almost
as Oscar
took the chance
to cuddle next to Yula
on a single cushion
reclining Goths rolled Rizlas
three tokes, Oscar's far out
drifting on a sonnet
Yula steered the barge
she'd sat by
down a Nile of corridor
towards the harbour
of her room

she raised her arms
her bead top floated down
landed with a shucking sound
she leant against the wall
took off her stout black boots
rolled down her witch-black tights
she had nothing else to lose
A virgin poet's hard to find
she pushed him down, ah, slow
took off his new-made clothes
he had plenty more to lose...

FOUR

Lorna's Block

In this condition
imagination
goes to live in shapes and colours
refuses
to creep into words...

Still Life

Elbows on the kitchen table
my outdoor shape slung crooked on a stool
pendant cone night-lighting, painting

an orange, nipples of lemon, two avocados
grand as emu's eggs, azalean
rising from terracotta bowl

Spode circle with rings of purpled onion
cubes of saffron cheese, tutu
of lettuce, greener than Lautrec's

a clump of bread, ragged, on oblong wood
rose in glass, my bucket bag
five chairs spindling into frame;

behind this screen
lost in memory, figures on a white page
struggle for dimension

Night Visitors

they feel their way inside from cars
through leaves blustering off trees
by foxes calling, owls hunting
someone pausing on the stairs;
argue in my ears in arcane words
moon-found, star-sharp, are utterly

at ease. I count them into cohorts, weave them
into paragrams; they swan about
trailing chevrons of light, inspire
my half-etched table and chair to croon
of forests, then settle into sand
under a quilted sea.

Eight o'clock floats up, a dull white pain
a door closes; they've gone

Glazed

My days are viscous, the sky
loiters near the ground, time tastes
unsalted, overcooked

drabness bloats my longing
for chocolate, I crave a cigarette
something alcoholic

the air is mid-beige, rancid
drifts in wry flavours above
old food, stacked dishes

I suck my teeth and pout
padding about, hating the room
its bric-a-brac

the dark stain on the wall
where I threw my wine
the night he left

I clench, sigh, sink
punch, switch, surf for blood
on the air

From the glazed box a hot
dazzle of gunfire spurts
in solidarity

violence beams at me
returns my stare, thinks it knows
who we really are.

Windows open inwards
beyond the glass a gang of dreams
plot among themselves...

Lost and Found

I'm running round the Rye
not just jogging
chasing people
I don't know where they've gone

Oscar's off with Yula somewhere
Mehmet's disappeared
Muscles got himself promoted
I feel terribly alone

They're pretending not to know me
when I ask them what they're doing
what they're going to do
they don't answer

they make me feel like someone's
nagging mother, kids grown up
and gone away, not even
leaving her a number

in the early hours they drop by
humming tunes I can't quite catch
disappear at daylight
my head is full of space

this park's enormous
so many places they could hide...

            I've collapsed
            under a willow

Be still Blake whispers
watch the leaves
they'll come back
never chase after people
see how the sunlight alters
tells you secrets, as it flutters
through the branches...

After a while I glimpse them
by the Butcher's Arms: Oscar
(thin these days) Yula, Mehmet
and a young man, cycling

FIVE

At the Butcher's Arms

We're round the Butcher's having a game pool right
in the boozer some div's looking for bother right
bother means bill
Angels ain't into bill
Angels is into pool like
having a jar

Matter of fact we ain't carrying no proof of age right
I clock the bill soon as they come through the door right
got out the way
in a flash like
shot upstairs for a piss
didn't I

Upstairs there's this room, load of weirdos right
this geezer spouting about Peckham like
why it ain't triffic, then again
why it is triffic
see what I mean
I thought he was talking to me
didn't I

Thing is, I know him, lives next door right
we always thought he was a div right
no bottle, no style
the Angels give him hassle
untold times, now
I see he's pukka
this geezer
name of Oscar

They're all shouting out, going *More!* right
the geezer won't give em more, sits down, sweet
this woman gets up
guess what
Lorna – my teacher!

she's alright
as it goes
she's on about some kid round the Centre right
name of Mem, doing cooking right
do me a favour!
And that bloke with the tail what reads meters
round the Burl, he's there, like
chirpsing Lorna

some skirt by the door hands me this book right
she goes, *Have it, it's poems, it's free* right
stuffs it in my pocket like
I might read *this* fucking book
as it goes... if... yeah, well
that's my problem, like...
see what I mean...

Deus Ex   Lorna is within writing distance

Musk and dewberry dropping down the walls
porous white clouds
cling round my knees, my breasts
the air is rich with heat and scent
my head feels calm

raising a tinted goblet to my lips
I sip a flowery wine
allow my thoughts to wander
through the misted mirror, stringing words
along a line, night birds

I sing them out; uncaged, they fly around
my empty house, chiming
inside the silence
The closest harmony is being alone...
there's a bell ringing

again, again, again. I gulp the wine
my birds begin to screech
blasphemous, obscene
Wrapping my steaming body in a towel
I footprint down the stairs

peer through the little spyglass in the door
am confronted by
a single cornflower eye
a steady gaze, a sweep of filament
across the lens

the eye moves back, becomes a slender shape
helmet in its hand
it bows and pirouettes
blond hair cascades about its neck, blazes
above the taut-zipped suit

I've seen this god somewhere, my palms perspire
I open up the door
May I bring it in?
a magical machine on latex wheels
he parks it in the hall

I indicate my towel, I was in...
I know, I know
as he unzips his suit
he has clairvoyant eyes, cool hands
    I've seen all this before...

Skin   Olly is within touching distance

Olly *had* known other skin, neutral
polite, against his palm, his cheek
medical skin, jabbing, swabbing
skin brushing, apologetic

This skin was geographic
skinscape of breast, belly, thighs
skin with smooth-talking fingers
questioning his ears, his lips

these fingers untied his moorings
raised mast and sails
unlocked his safe inland canals
coxswained him to sea

these fingers beckoned lost words
released them to the wind
rollicked Olly's barge, rode him
into fierce dark water

these words were fingers
pushing him overboard
the supple skin of dolphins
diving and swimming...

Her storm-cloud hair rose and fell,
Oscar! White reefs parted
his skin was wave, rolling, rolling, oceans
washed away the sound of his name
Olly gone   Oscar home

And morning come, dusty London
sloping through a beaded sash
Oscar wakes, puts his glasses on
focusses the miracle of skin

A meter reader chains his bike
against the Lido fence
sits under a tree
eating his sandwiches
watching the branches
flexing in the sun

Reading Mehmet

How do you know
what the inside of water's like?
Only water
knows what the inside of water's like
and water can't tell you

How do you know
what the insides of words is like?
Like putting your head in a computer?
You might never get out,
know what I mean...

How do *you* know
what not reading's like?
A world of pen and ink drawings
abstract, safe, like not opening
Pandora's box?

Mem had enough people shouting at him
without words doing it an' all
but Lorna's been putting him into words
he has to know

She's told him about syllables, vowels, all that stuff
he understands, not that hard
bit like breaking into a motor
easy as piss, it's just...

you can feel the oil, the hot metal, the rust
the spanner loosening off the nut
without getting your hands dirty...
has to be a plus

Everywhere he goes he reads the signs
who knows if he reads them better
now he's broken into words?

Muscles at the Hub

Life on target, yup, he's been short-listed
relaxed, he fires syllables towards the panel
Market-driven re-alignment as required. Bingo!

Muscles moves from Camberwell to Bromley
Sundays, fusses round a suave new car
his feet go left, right, right, right to the top

Head of education, head of leisure
head of finance, head of demolition
committed to committees, king of cuts

Brum, brum, the tuned-up engine purrs
he cruises into Surrey, climbs to ninety
fights a corner – skree...e...e...chkn...vrrr...

> His dad, track-knackered, boilersuited
> would shout, *Upstairs you idle git*
> *no grub for you until your homework's done*
>
> *we've given up our lives, me and your mum*
> *pay now, live later, always been our motto*
> *you'll get a thump if all that work's not done*

Muscles in the fast lane overtaking, vrrrooooom
A conference in Brighton – 'Raising Standards'
the buzz words: discipline, curriculum

Back at the office boots the Apple, beep, beep
spends the night with spreadsheets, re-devising
a cost-effective service, geared to budget

He's left her in the carpark in his place
THIS SPACE RESERVED FOR HEAD OF ... everything!
Everyone sees her shimmering curves, (va va voom!)... are his

Meg Peach Leaving

Meg Peach is sitting by her window
waiting for the meals on wheels to come
she don't look forward to them dinners
slopping gravy with a plastic spoon

Some days she sees her hubby's face, he looks
like Bert but still got all his hair
she don't look forward to them baths
the nurses washing her down there

Someone's standing at the gate
must be mum, got back from the draper's
all pins and bustle, no not her
that fair chap come to read the meter

What's that bell? must be Tom again
come back on leave, come on the tram
brought his kitbag home with him
what's that bell, it must be time...it must be time...

Mehmet's Haiku   (for Lorna)

Experiences

First
that red chair round nan's
she put a cushion on it
give me pink ice-cream

Worst
the worst thing was when
that git what got off with mum
come to live with us

Best
she weren't mine but she
let me take her and drive her
away – she's blinding

Funniest
letting down the tyres
of Muscles car at home time
on rainy Fridays

Matter of Fact

Seventeen
ain't enough syllables
you need a mouthful
like bastard and tosser
and untold more
(but Lorna might get mad)

That fucker kept me in detention
made me write *I must remember*
to wear a blue striped tie to school
he made me write it fifty times
I'll give him stripes; I ain't got no ties
my mum says ties don't grow on trees
she needs the dosh for wonderloaves
sugar, burgers; she gets me T-shirts, jeans
Nikes, no one don't wear ties!
I hate that grin of his
way he drums his fingers on the desk, goes
Not one of life's high fliers are we Mehmet

He said I'd writ '*remember*' wrong
left out '*me*', he made me write it all again
fifty times, tore it up didn't he
chucked it in the bin. That's when I hit him

Get this! Lorna says he's chief
of education now, wrestling with the cuts
I'll give him wrestle, I'll give him cuts
he's going to close our Centre
I'll give him centre – right between the eyes!

Seventeen syllables
ain't enough
to give Muscles
what he deserves
he needs a ton of em
brick ones – right in the balls

Lorna laughed
when I give it in,
she goes *Well done, Mem*
I never thought
you could write so much

Olly to Oscar

Is this me, dark green shirt on
with just a hint of chic
I look thin, I'm not the same
where's my barge, my bags
what's my name?

She thinks that I'm successful, poet
of the local scene
cool, clever, popular
she calls out in the night
I love you, Oscar

She hasn't seen that hopeless other
hiding in the flat
hoping nobody will notice
clumsy Olly, laureate
of cockroaches

Everybody has an Olly
in the heart, cramped
starved of light – but virgin poets
are rare as Rye Lane pearls
she knows it

We're changing places, swapping sets
me, the actor, outside
Olly safe within, guardian
of fear and feeling
Oscar – the man

Oscar Peckham, fully-fledged
stunning plimmers flying
past the Lido, in a swirl
of leaves and stars
to meet his girl

Lookin' at you Kid   In praise of younger men

His jeans don't have to support
his belly, the hems
rest on hunky DMs

He has left his father's closet
where sad suits hung like shrouds
in camphor clouds

He'll pose, artless as a butterfly
round his svelte body he'll throw
my kimono

He conjures intimate soul feasts
from peppers, pulses and stock
magicked in a wok

He will light scented candles to me
make love in their sensuous glow
does he know

I adore looking at him?
I just wish he
would stop looking at me

Angel Occupations

What shall we do today!
Break in and drive away!
        Muscles can take the bus
        this car belongs to us
        scratch it up and make it run
        give the bill a bit of fun
        give the gears a lot of gyp
        leave it round the council tip
What shall we do today
Take it! And drive away

[crime: seems to be a form of play]

Steppin' Out

If they were Fred and Ginger
they would dance onto the platforms
of the buses that are dawdling down Rye Lane
with the bus queue at the bus stop
harmonisin' barbershop
while the waiters at the Jade Star would be swayin'
           boo boop i doop, voh di o doh
they'd spring onto the sidewalk
with a tap step and a shuffle
and Fred would catch his top hat on his cane
if they were Fred and Ginger
they would sing a bit of Gershwin
while off the set the orchestra is playin'
           boo boop i doop, voh di o doh
If they were Fred and Ginger
he would buy red roses for her
and pin them on her sequins like a flame
while the coster by his barrow
would exclaim, *Lor luv yer Guvner*
and the customers would join in the refrain
           boo boop i doop, voh di o doh
Then they'd waltz off to the Ritz
with a chassee and a shimmy
and Fred would stretch his arms out like a plane
if they were Fred and Ginger
they would fall in love forever
and never know another moment's pain
           boo boop i doop, voh di o doh
Oscar steppin' out with Yula
only going shopping, but
they feel like Fred and Ginger all the time
           boo oop i doop voh di o doh
           boo oop I doop voh di o day

SIX

boo boop i doop, vo di o day
take it and drive away!

[crime: rough place to play]

Down Choumert Road

there's daffs, a quid three bunches
new season's spuds, thirty pence a pound
six limes fifty pence, fresh crimson chillies
capers, cardamoms, cumin, puzzles of ginger
eddoes, mangos, melons, ackee, chow chow
pale dimpled breadfruit, manioc rough as bark

fans of skate on marble, shark fin, turbot
huss, bass, goat-fish, ink-fish in a bucket,
Goes well with custard, want some parsley with it?
His rubbers slub a nifty riff, *Here George*
he scuds a mullet; rhythm's pummelling on
from Blue Beat City – Rap and Ragga, Reggae
Hip-Hop, Ska; *Not like the old days*
is it, Mrs Lady? He winks, *You won't remember,*
cabbage, cod on Friday, forever Crosby
crooning Easter Bonnet on the wireless

Outside the Wishing Well

        down Choumert Road, the four of us
Oscar with his Yula,
my lover gazing: *meet her read her*
Oscar's moving to the squat tomorrow
he's working on an ode to Thomas Crapper's
delicate blue roses
Yula's smile is brilliant
April's here

Down the road
a hearse appears
spring flowers crafted into MUM
shoppers pause, look shifty, carry on
filling their bags with greens
some old lady
just missed a telegram

A car shoots round the corner, sporty
Muscles' car, it skids, revolves
mounts the Roller
guess who's driving?

The bones of ninety-nine-year-old Meg Peach
are catapaulted through the far-end door
a hellish Jaguar mouth consumes them

The tarmac teams with fruit and white carnations
MUM falls to pieces, pale Angel faces
on the kerb, shoppers standing
ambulances bleeping, bill with tapes
my young god offering the kiss of life
*This one's a gone*r says a paramedic

In the gutter by an apple, a flimsy notebook
it says, *Mehmet ...IQs ... for Lorna*

OUTRO

It's my last flight, Monday morning
             sun rising out of Lewisham
          trees in blossom, dew flashing
                 Rye geese are breakfasting

        roar of Concorde above, below me
                 trucks and cars are inching
                 into town. A big red crane
             draws level, cranking, shifting

            hanging above the Lido, waiting;
           in its cab a man is smoking roll-ups
              drinking a pint-sized mug of tea
                 a dusty roll of cloud is rising

                Muscles in a suit and hard hat
             inspects below; he dreams the Rye
                 is like a ship, his ship, arriving
                 cutting a giant wave, cleansing

              the littered streets, sleazy pubs
                 greasy caffs, sailing towards
             millennium, steering Peckham up
               the fast lane of the super-highway

           He'll found a William Blake Centre
                 paid for by the lottery: *a world
             in a stretch of land*, he wonders
          where he's heard that phrase before

        I dive lower, on the trees are stickers
           SAVE OUR PARK, GET MUSCLES
             a lead ball hits the swimming pool
          leaves fly up, the dust cloud billows
             a metal lobster's shovelling broken
                concrete, a wheel, an old shield
          a rusty dagger, all gone for hardcore
     a falling star sparks past...
                       a dogend

Other books by Hylda Sims:

Inspecting the Island – *the Summerhill Novel*, Seven-Ply Yarns, 2000

Sayling the Babel – poems and songs, Hearing Eye, 2006

Waterwords – Lido Poems (mostly by children, written at Brockwell Lido pool, London, SE24), BLUpress, 2008 co-edited with Melanie Mauthner

www.hylda.co.uk